How do you like ou

We would really appreciate you leav

Other Picture Books:

For other fun Picture Books by Kampelstone, simply search for:

Kampelstone Picture Books

Copyright© 2020 by Kampelstone. All rights reserved.
This book or any portion thereof may not be reproduced or used in any manner whatsoever without the express written permission of the publisher.

INTERESTING FACTS ABOUT HUNGARY

- The word Hungary traces its roots to an old Oghut-Turkic word 'Onogur' which means the ten tribes of the Ogurs. The people themselves refer to one of the main original semi-nomadic tribes of people who settled the area called the Magyeri.

- The people of Hungary call themselves Magyar and not Hungarian.

- The crowning of Arpad, first king of the Magyars marked the beginning of the Hungarian state in 896.

- As a nod to the 'birth' year of the country in 896, Budapest built their metro on the millennial anniversary in 1896. As well, buildings in Budapest must not exceed 96 meters (315 feet) or roughly the height of London's Big Ben clock tower. And the Hungarian national anthem should be sung in 96 seconds if sung at the proper tempo.

- The Budapest metro began operations in 1896. It is the second oldest electrically operated underground railway in the world, predated only by the London Underground.

- At nearly 230 square miles (600 square kilometers), Lake Balaton is the largest lake in Central Europe. It is often referred to as the Hungarian Sea and has always been a popular sunbathing and swimming area.

- All together, Hungary has more than thirteen hundred hot springs and there are at least 450 public spas and bathhouses. Each spring has varying quantities of dissolved minerals so each spa is different.

- There is a legend that if a person touches the pen of the statue of Anonymous in Budapest's City Park, that person will be blessed with great writing abilities.

- Hungary's Tokaj region has been producing win for a thousand years. The wines are particularly sweet because they have been affected by noble rot, a type of spore which alters and sweetens the wine grapes. The nectar from the grapes of Tokaj are mentioned in Hungary's national anthem.

- Erich Weisz, the illusionist who went by the stage name Harry Houdini, was born in Budapest in 1874.

- Judit Polgar, considered to be the strongest female chess player of all time, acquired the title of grand-master in 1991 when she was only fifteen. Chess is extremely popular amongst Hungarians and is played everywhere, even on floating boards while swimming.

- More than 1,000 tons of the spice paprika are produced annually in Hungary. There are two paprika museums, Szeged and Molnar, which give an insight into the industry as well as a spicy sample.

- The world's largest geothermal cave system is just underneath Budapest, the capital city and includes 200 subterranean chambers.

- Movie production greats Adolf Zukor, founder of Paramount Pictures, Mano Kaminer (Michael Curtiz) director of Casablanca and Vilmos Fried (William Fox), founder of Fox studios, were all born in Hungary.

- The Gyermekvasut Railway that runs through Buda hills between Széchenyi Hill and Hűvösvölgy stations is run almost exclusively by 10 to 14 year-olds from local schools who make up the ticket sellers and conductors, man the switch points and sell station memorabilia.

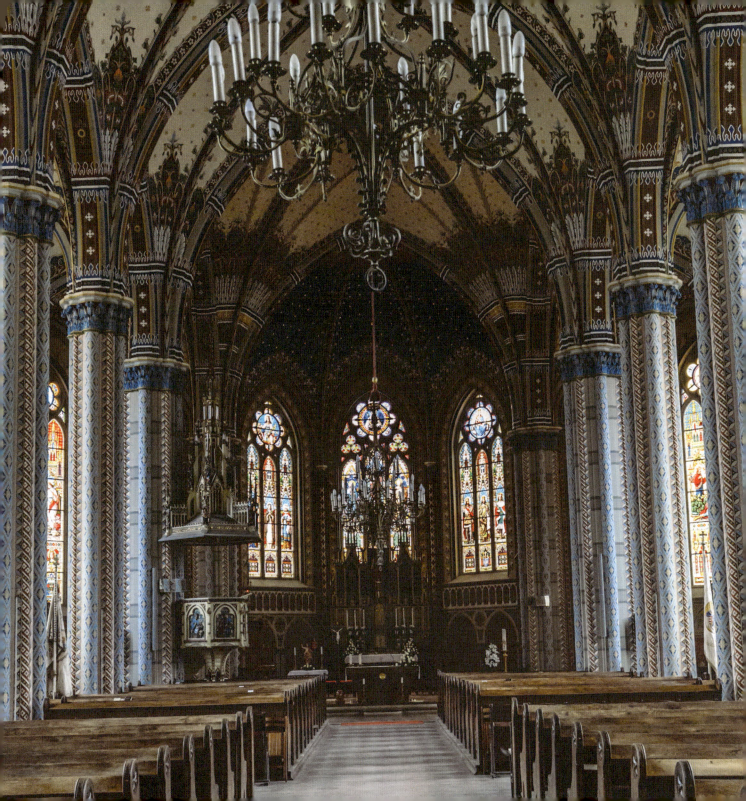

Printed in Great Britain
by Amazon